Answering the
Questions of Jesus

Fr. Andrew Apostoli, CFR

Answering the Questions of Jesus

EWTN PUBLISHING, INC.
Irondale, Alabama

EWTN Publishing, Inc.
5817 Old Leeds Road, Irondale, AL 35210

Distributed by Sophia Institute Press
Box 5284, Manchester, NH 03108

Library of Congress Cataloging-in-Publication Data

Names: Apostoli, Andrew, author.
Title: Answering the questions of Jesus / Fr. Andrew Apostoli.
Description: Irondale, Alabama : EWTN Publishing, Inc., 2016.
Identifiers: LCCN 2016020925 | ISBN 9781682780169 (pbk. : alk. paper)
Subjects: LCSH: Jesus Christ—Teachings—Miscellanea. | Questioning. |
    Catholic Church—Doctrines.
Classification: LCC BS2415 .A66 2016 | DDC 232.9/54—dc23 LC record
available at https://lccn.loc.gov/2016020925

First printing

*Dedicated with deep love and gratitude
to the Sacred Heart of Jesus
and the Immaculate Heart of Mary.
May they bless all who read this book.*

Contents

Introduction

I greet you with a greeting of St. Francis: "May the Lord give you His peace!"

From His teenage years through His Ascension, questions were central to the way Jesus spread the gospel. In fact, the very first words of Our Lord that are recorded in Scripture were questions. When His parents found Him teaching the elders in the Temple, He responded, "How is it that you sought me? Did you not know that I must be in my Father's house?" (Luke 2:49; see chapter 1 of this book).

Sometimes Jesus used questions to quiz His followers about the Truth He was preaching, such as when He asked His Apostles, "[W]ho do you say that

I am?" (Matthew 16:15; see chapter 6). Sometimes His questions were expressions of frustration, such as when He asked Peter, James, and John in the Garden of Gethsemane, "Could you not watch with me one hour?" (Matthew 26:40; see chapter 11). And sometimes Jesus' questions seem to be directed directly at you and me, such as when He asked the Apostles on the stormy Sea of Galilee, "Why are you afraid? Have you no faith?" (Mark 4:40; see chapter 4).

What all these questions have in common is that we can still learn so much from them today.

First, we can learn about Jesus' ministry. Looking at His questions is a wonderful way of entering into the Gospel stories. Each question will allow us to go deeper into understanding the way Jesus went about His time on earth.

After all, a consistent teaching of Pope Francis has been that our Faith is found not just in lists of doctrines, but in relationship with a person: Jesus Christ. What better way to deepen that relationship than to enter into conversation with Him? And what better way to enter into conversation with Jesus than to answer the questions He asked throughout His ministry?

And that is the second part of examining the questions of Jesus: asking ourselves how we would answer Him. Understanding Jesus is one thing. Knowing Him, as a friend, is another. I hope you'll use these reflections not just to understand Him better, but to know Him better.

Together, we can grow to appreciate more fully the wisdom, the message, and the Person of Jesus.

May God bless you.

Answering the
Questions of Jesus

⤙

Did You Not Know That I Must Be in My Father's House?

The very first questions of Jesus occur when Mary and Joseph find their twelve-year-old son in the Temple in Jerusalem, teaching the teachers. Let's start with some background.

The Holy Family went to Jerusalem every year for the feast of Passover. After the feast was over, they left to return home to Nazareth in Galilee, which was a three-day journey. When they would travel in those days, the men would be in one group and the women in another; the children could go with either parent. Mary apparently thought that Jesus was with

Joseph, and Joseph thought that He was with Mary. After a whole day's journey, they came together for the evening and realized their son wasn't with either of them. They looked among their relatives and acquaintances and did not find Him.

They traced their steps back to Jerusalem to look for Him: "After three days they found him in the temple, sitting among the teachers, listening to them and asking them questions. All who heard him were amazed at his understanding and his answers" (Luke 2:46–47).

You can imagine the relief of parents who have lost a child! We tend to think of Mary and Joseph as almost angelic figures, totally different from ourselves, but the truth is that all the human concerns and emotions that any parents would experience overwhelmed them. Is He safe? Does He have something to eat? Does He have a place to sleep?

As the story continues Jesus speaks His first words in Scripture:

And when they saw him they were astonished; and his mother said to him, "Son, why have you treated us so? Behold, your father and I have been looking for you anxiously." And he said to them, "How is it that you sought me? Did you not know that I must be in my Father's house?" And they did not understand the saying which he spoke to them. (Luke 2:48–50)

Now, Jesus is not asking His Mother why she was upset about losing Him. That's a natural emotion that any parent is going to feel, and Jesus understands that. He is, after all, fully human as well as fully divine. We should read that question in the context of His second question. What Jesus is asking, then, was why His parents didn't go directly to the Temple ("His Father's house") instead of searching for Him.

St. Luke sums up this event by telling us, "He went down with them and came to Nazareth, and was obedient to them; and his mother kept all these things in her heart. And Jesus increased in wisdom and in stature, and in favor with God and man" (Luke 2:51–52). It is clear that Mary did not understand what Jesus was trying to accomplish with His questions, which was to lead her and Joseph to a deeper understanding of His identity.

The key to this dialogue is the ambiguity of the term *Father*. When Mary says "your father and I," she is obviously referring to St. Joseph, the earthly father of Jesus. Although Joseph didn't beget Jesus, in every other way he was a father to Him. He was provider and protector, and he was the true spouse of Mary. But Jesus, in responding to Mary, is referring to His Heavenly Father when he mentions His "Father's house." Our Lord was leading His parents to understand more deeply His dual identity as their earthly son and the Son of the Eternal Father.

Although His parents could not grasp what He was saying, Mary never stopped reflecting on His words. Our Lady was, as St. Augustine said, not only Jesus' Mother but also His disciple. Every disciple of Jesus must grow not only in faith, hope, and love, but also in understanding of who the Lord is. This is what Jesus was encouraging in His parents.

Let's look at how this affects our own lives — how our discipleship can be seen in Mary and Joseph's experience in the Gospel story.

Where Do We Find Jesus?

When I teach about prayer, I incorporate St. John of the Cross's teaching on the Dark Night of the Soul—periods of spiritual dryness we experience as we grow in prayer and holiness. St. John tells us there are actually two distinct experiences: the Dark Night of the Senses and, later on, as we reach the highest stages of prayer, the Dark Night of the Spirit.

The Dark Night of the Senses is like Mary and Joseph's loss of the Child Jesus. The Dark Night of the Spirit, on the other hand, is like Mary's agony at the foot of the Cross. But our focus here is on the former.

In the Dark Night of the Senses, three things happen. First, we experience a loss of the feeling of God. For example, until this point we may have enjoyed much consolation from prayer, a good feeling in the heart made us feel assured God was near and was watching over us. But St. John of the Cross would say that when we go through the Dark Night of the Senses, it seems as if the presence of Jesus is abruptly taken away, just like Mary and Joseph's losing the Child Jesus. This is the loss of the feeling of God.

The second experience in the Dark Night of the Senses is feeling unable to pray, as, when Jesus was missing, Mary and Joseph couldn't talk to Him. But the third experience St. John of the Cross talks about is the most important: a great, continuing desire to want to love God. And, of course, for Mary and Joseph there is a burning desire to find the Child Jesus.

I'm sure you have felt some of the feelings of spiritual dryness St. John of the Cross describes — a sudden loss of the feeling of Jesus' presence, loss of the consolation of prayer, and yet a deep desire to want God. Maybe you've actually been through the Dark Night of the Senses without knowing it. You wanted the Lord but didn't know where He was.

When Jesus asks His parents why they didn't go directly to His "Father's house," He is first of all, as we've said, revealing His relationship to His Heavenly Father. He continues to be Mary and Joseph's son; as we saw in the Gospel, He went back to Nazareth and "was obedient to them." Jesus spent thirty years at the home in Nazareth with His earthly family, preparing for His mission to save the world. He was formed in that family environment. But He was also the Son of the Eternal Father. His parents can't quite grasp this, but Mary ponders it in her heart.

Shouldn't we do that? Don't we need the Holy Spirit to enlighten us so that we can understand the mysteries of God? Do we understand Him as our Savior? Do we acknowledge that He's the One Who saves us from our sins? The One Who gives us the grace we need to live our Christian life every day, to practice the virtues we need to be true disciples?

But there's a second takeaway from these questions of Jesus: He is telling us where to find Him. Do we find Him, for instance, in the Eucharist? When we are at Mass, are we conscious of Jesus' presence there? Do we prepare our minds and hearts to receive Him in Holy Communion? Do we visit Him in the church? Do we understand that He is always in His "Father's house" because Christ dwells in all our churches in the Blessed Sacrament?

Where else can we find Him? We can encounter God in solitude, in silence and prayer alone with Him.

When we read His Word and meditate on the Gospels, He is there; after all, He is the Eternal Word. And we find Him in our own hearts. If we are living in the state of grace, the Lord is with us.

Finally, we can find Jesus—and He doesn't want us to miss Him here—in the poor and the vulnerable. Remember that Jesus said, "[A]s you did it to one of the least of these my brethren, you did it to me"(Matthew 25:40). Mother Teresa, in her own beautiful way, reminded us that Jesus is present in the poorest of the poor. At the end of the Divine Praises during Benediction, her Missionaries of Charity add this petition: "Blessed be Jesus in the poorest of the poor."

We can find the Lord in so many places as long as we know that we're looking for Him—whether it is in our churches, in our prayers, in His Word in our hearts, or in the poorest of the poor. Once we find Him, as we will see in the next question of Jesus, it is our responsibility to stay with Him and to bring Him to others.

⁀

Questions for Reflection and Discussion

- How can I grow in my understanding of who Jesus is?

- Have I experienced a Dark Night of the Senses, when the feeling of the presence of Jesus fades away?

- Where in my everyday life can I find Jesus?

- How would I respond to this question of Jesus if it were addressed directly to me: "Did you not know that I must be in my Father's house?"

What Do You Seek?

It's so important to know where to find Jesus in our lives; but do we really understand what (and *Whom*) we're looking for? This is the next question in the Gospel that we find Jesus asking two of His future Apostles: "What do you seek?" (John 1:38).

This story takes place after Jesus' Baptism by St. John the Baptist in the Jordan River. The Baptism of Jesus marks the end of His hidden life at Nazareth. Let's start exploring this question of Jesus by exploring His Baptism.

The baptism of John was not our sacramental Baptism. John's baptism could not take away sins; only Jesus' Baptism can, because Jesus has the power to forgive sins. John's baptism was just a sign of a new life of repentance.

But Jesus came for John's baptism even though He had no sins to repent of. John even says, "I need to be baptized by you" (Matthew 3:14). Our Lord insisted, though, and went down into the waters of the Jordan — waters that had become spiritually polluted by the sins of those who had confessed and repented there. Jesus took those sins upon Himself. As Isaiah the prophet said, He "has borne" our sins (Isaiah 53:4); that is why He suffered.

As He did this, He purified the waters and gave them, in His Baptism, the power to take away sins. To this day, if a priest or deacon baptizes using water from the Jordan River, he doesn't have to bless the water, since it was blessed by Christ two thousand years ago.

As Jesus emerged from His Baptism, two things happened. First, a voice spoke out: "This is my beloved Son, with whom I am well pleased" (Matthew 3:17). The Father is speaking, revealing His Son. At the same time, St. John tells us that he saw the Holy Spirit descend as a dove and land on Jesus (John 1:32). In other words, Jesus was anointed by the Holy Spirit for

His mission as the Messiah (which means "anointed one"). He was now filled with the Holy Spirit to bring to others in His mission as the Savior of the world.

It's with that background that we pick up the story in the Gospel of John:

> The next day again John was standing with two of his disciples; and he looked at Jesus as he walked, and said, "Behold, the Lamb of God!" The two disciples heard him say this, and they followed Jesus. Jesus turned, and saw them following, and said to them, "What do you seek?" And they said to him, "Rabbi" (which means Teacher), "where are you staying?" He said to them, "Come and see." They came and saw where he was staying; and they stayed with him that day, for it was about the tenth hour. (John 1:35–39)

These two disciples of John the Baptist are my patron saint: St. Andrew the Apostle and an unnamed man traditionally assumed to be St. John the Apostle. When the Baptist points out Jesus as the Messiah, they leave the Baptist and begin to follow Jesus.

Note what Andrew and John say when the Lord asks what they're looking for: they ask where He is staying. Isn't that what we should be looking for, too — to find out where we can find Jesus and be with Him? And in response He gives that beautiful invitation: "Come and see."

From this moment on, Andrew and John stayed with Jesus. The Old Testament practice was that disciples stayed with their rabbi, their teacher, as long as the rabbi could teach them something, at which point they would go out on their own to become rabbis in their own right. But when it comes to being a disciple of Jesus, we don't leave Him. We don't leave His message, which is inexhaustible. We don't start teaching our own truths or our own opinions. We must always teach what the Lord has given us. We must always remain with Him, just as Andrew and John did. It's by being with Jesus that we too are transformed.

Looking for — and Finding — Jesus

What if Jesus asked you what you were looking for? What would you answer Him?

Let's use Mass as an example. What are we looking for in the Mass? Are we just fulfilling an obligation? That's not a really deep motivation, is it? We must seek the Person of Jesus!

Maybe we just go to church out of routine, hardly ever considering why we're showing up at Mass each Sunday. A group once told me that their church always has a big crowd for the Saturday evening Mass because people want to get to the restaurants first that evening. That's a sign we're following something or someone else ahead of Jesus.

We must seek the real reason for going to Mass: to share in Jesus' Sacrifice at the altar and to worship the Lord. The first purpose of our worship is to adore God. We adore Him for Who He is: all good and worthy of all of our love. Secondly, we seek His mercy because we are sorry for our sins. We express that sorrow knowing that in the Mass God bestows His grace of mercy upon us. And lastly, in worship we give thanks to God for His blessings.

These three reasons to seek God in the Mass — adoration, contrition, and thanksgiving — are really three of the purposes of all prayer. We can also add a fourth: prayer to petition God for the things we really need for ourselves, for our families, for our mission in life, and for the life of the Church: prayers for vocations to the priesthood and religious life, for our clergy, for the Holy Father and the bishops, for missions, for conversion, and for peace in the world and an end of the culture of death. For these and other concerns in our life, we must seek God first.

There are so many reasons why we should want to come to Jesus; this question helps us to deepen our understanding of our reasons for seeking Him. Let's see what happens after the initial encounter with Jesus:

> One of the two who heard John speak, and followed him, was Andrew, Simon Peter's brother. He first found his brother Simon, and said to him, "We have found the Messiah" (which means Christ). He brought him to Jesus. Jesus looked at him, and said, "So you are Simon the son of John? You shall be called Cephas" (which means Peter). (John 1:40–42)

Andrew's reaction to being with Jesus was not only to stay with Him that day, but to go out and become a wonderful recruiter. (Bishop Fulton Sheen referred to St. Andrew as the public-relations man among the Apostles.) This is important: we can't bring people to Jesus if we don't know where to find Him. How can we bring people to the Eucharist if we ourselves do not appreciate Jesus' presence in that Eucharist? We have to know the Lord and where to find Him so we can bring others to Him. That's what Andrew did.

What will we do after going to Mass on Sunday, for example? Will we go out and share the message of Jesus with others? Has our experience at Mass changed us and made us want to be better disciples of Jesus? If it has, we have something very important to bring to the world. If it hasn't, we've missed what it's all about.

Many people say they don't "get anything" out of Mass. Bishop Sheen used to say that's because they didn't put anything into it! We have to put our love into our worship. We have to look for Jesus and stay with Him, as Andrew and John did. We have the mission to bring people to Jesus, but we have to experience change within ourselves in order to become true evangelists. That's why it's very important for us not to forget that we are disciples of Jesus.

Answering the Questions of Jesus

One of the greatest saints in the history of the Church is St. Bernard of Clairvaux. He used to bring so many recruits to the religious life that a saying about him developed: "When Bernard came around to preach, the mothers hid their sons, the girlfriends hid their boyfriends, and the wives hid their husbands." He had a little sign on his desk, though, to remind him to examine his motivations and remember his true mission: "Bernard, why have you come here?"

We need to keep asking ourselves this question, because once we find what we're looking for — a relationship with the living God — we have to preserve it. How do we do that? We build on it every day, through prayer and acts of love. Remember the words of Yogi Berra: "It ain't over till it's over." Our discipleship is not over until Jesus calls us. Then we will be with the Lord and He will say to us the words He says in the Gospel: "Well done, good and faithful servant; ... enter into the joy of your master" (Matthew 25:23).

Those are the words each one of us should be longing to hear from Jesus. Imagine: to be in His presence for all eternity. And that eternity can begin right now as we seek the Lord and get to know Him. If we tell the Lord, as Andrew and John did, that we want to know where He is staying, the Lord will invite us to come and be with Him.

~

Questions for Reflection and Discussion

- Do I stay with Jesus always, or do I follow other teachers — the culture, the media, and other distractions — when it is convenient?

- How can I prepare myself better for Mass as an encounter with Jesus, not just an obligation?

- What opportunities do I have in my daily life to bring people to Jesus?

- How would I respond to this question of Jesus if it were addressed directly to me: "What do you seek?"

~

Woman, What Concern Is That to You and to Me?

Jesus' next question — the second question asked of His Mother — occurs at the wedding feast at Cana. This is a very important moment because it leads to tremendous consequences: Jesus will work His first miracle, and His disciples will really begin to believe in Him.

Let's look at the Gospel of St. John:

> On the third day there was a wedding in Cana of Galilee, and the mother of Jesus was there. Jesus and his disciples had also been invited to the wedding. When the wine gave out, the

mother of Jesus said to him, "They have no wine." And Jesus said to her, "Woman, what concern is that to you and to me? My hour has not yet come." (John 2:1–4, NRSV)

Now, Jewish wedding celebrations sometime lasted for as long as a week. That meant that there had to be a lot of wine. They didn't drink water in those days, but they did drink an awful lot of wine!

Mary notices the wine is running out, and she feels a concern that this young couple will be embarrassed, so she simply makes it known to Jesus. Mary's request, simple as it is, is filled with great trust and expectation. She expects Jesus to do something — and she's not expecting Him to go out and buy a barrel of wine. She is demonstrating that she now understands His identity more deeply than she did when she found Him in the Temple. No doubt the Holy Spirit had helped her to realize the full identity of Christ as not only her son but also the Eternal Father's Son — fully human and fully divine.

Jesus' response is very interesting. First, He calls His Mother "Woman." There is no other known example in ancient Greek or Jewish writings of a man ever calling his own mother "woman." No doubt it's a reference back to Genesis, where God speaks to the serpent after he has deceived our first parents, Adam and Eve: "I will put enmity between you and the woman" (Genesis 3:15). And so Mary is the new Eve. With her assent, salvation comes to the world, undoing Eve's assent to the devil.

But Jesus is saying something even more. By saying that His "hour has not yet come," He is telling Mary that this moment will initiate His journey to the Cross. Our Blessed Lord is telling His Mother that if He does this miracle, He will be on His way to His Passion, death, and Resurrection.

This sounds, therefore, almost like a rebuke of His Mother. Mary, though, does not take it that way: "His mother said to the servants, 'Do whatever he tells you'" (John 2:5, NRSV). It is Mary, then, who affirms that it is time for Jesus to reveal Himself. Bishop Sheen asked, "What mother would ever send her own son onto a battlefield?" The answer, of course, is one who trusts God, her Son, and His mission: to redeem the world.

Those are also the Blessed Mother's last words recorded in Scripture. And what good ones they are! Nothing could be more important for us than to do whatever Jesus tells us.

The passage continues:

Now standing there were six stone water jars for the Jewish rites of purification, each holding twenty or thirty gallons. Jesus said to them, "Fill the jars with water." And they filled them up to the brim. He said to them, "Now draw some out, and take it to the chief steward." So they took it. When the steward tasted the water that had become wine, and did not know where it came from (though the servants who had drawn the water knew), the steward called the bridegroom and said to him, "Everyone serves the good wine first, and then the inferior wine after the guests have become drunk. But you have kept the good wine until now." Jesus did this, the first of his signs, in Cana of Galilee, and revealed his glory; and his disciples believed in him. (John 2:6–11, NRSV)

With this miracle we see a prefiguring of the Eucharist, when Jesus takes the cup of wine at the Last Supper and changes it into His Precious Blood. Jesus reveals His power at Cana, setting His path toward the Last Supper, when He will even more beautifully "manifest His glory" by changing that wine into His Precious Blood—the price of our salvation.

Praying with Perseverance

Now, what can we learn for our own lives from this episode? Jesus, as He did for His own Mother, will often give us responses that test our faith. But Mary doesn't stop when Jesus seems to avoid her request. Her faith, trust, and love are so deep that she tells the servers to do whatever Jesus tells them. She won't take no for an answer. Her faith teaches us that when we approach the Lord we must have that same kind of faith and trust in His goodness. The Little Flower, St. Thérèse of Lisieux, said that we get from God what we expect. And Mary expected her son to do something incredible to replenish the wine.

When we pray, do we easily give up? At the first sign of a no, do we shut down our prayer? Or do we persevere? Jesus said, "Ask, and it will be given you" (Matthew 7:7), but He didn't say to ask just once. We have to keep on asking. In that same verse, He said, "[S]eek, and you will find," but He didn't tell us, "Seek for three minutes; if you don't find anything, you can give up." He said, "[K]nock, and [the door] will be opened to you," but sometimes you have to keep on knocking until the person inside hears it.

The Lord often tells us to pray with perseverance. In the Gospels, Jesus tells two stories that illustrate the point: the story of the man knocking on his neighbor's door late at night and the story of the woman pleading with the corrupt judge to hear her case (Luke 11:5–13; 18:1–8). In other words, the Lord is telling us to annoy Him!

God hears all prayers, but He answers them in different ways. St. Augustine tells us there are three reasons why God may say no to our prayers. First, we can ask for the wrong things — things that are bad for us. God as a loving Father is not going to give us something that will harm us. We may pray, for instance, to win the lottery. God may know, however, that winning the lottery would do us spiritual harm.

Secondly, we might be living the wrong kind of life. Now, God does hear the prayers of unrepentant sinners, and He does sometimes give them a favorable answer so as to draw them to His goodness. But that's not always the case. God listens to those who listen to Him. We should be trying to live a good life, following God's law, if we really want Him to answer our prayers.

And finally, we can ask in the wrong way. We saw Mary respond to Jesus with perseverance. Do we pray with that kind of trust? Do we truly believe that God loves us enough to hear our prayer? He hears the prayers of all who pray with that childlike trust and commitment.

Even when God says yes to our prayers, though, it doesn't always feel like it. His answers come at different rates of speed. I like to compare three ways God responds to three ways we cook a meal: microwave, stovetop, and Crock-Pot.

The microwave reminds me of prayers to St. Anthony. I lose a lot of things. But after searching and searching for hours and maybe even days, I say a prayer to St. Anthony, and boom! there it is. I've had that experience many times. A microwave answer to your prayer, then, can be sudden and unexpected.

Sometimes, though, our prayers have to cook for a little while. If you're praying for something to happen tomorrow, it's not going to happen today; rather, it will happen in its proper time. Sometimes, though, the proper time is known only to God; it's up to us to trust Him.

But then there are prayers that have to sit in the Crock-Pot — or slow cooker — for a long time. There are some graces that are so important that God has to prepare them — and us — for a long time. He can't rush them, and neither can we.

I often think of the example of St. Monica praying for the conversion of her son, St. Augustine, for sixteen years. St. Augustine writes in his *Confessions* that the floor in the church where his mother prayed for him was wet with tears. God took a long time, but the results were world changing. Millions and millions of people have been impacted by St. Augustine — and also by the example of his mother.

Finally, God may not give us exactly what we ask for, but something even more beautiful in its place. This is where a lot of our disappointments come in life; it is sometimes at these moments that our faith is tested the most. It is up to us to try to see the reasons for what God presents us with — and to trust Him even if we can't figure it out. I know that in my life, and I'm sure in yours as well, it is often only in retrospect that I can truly appreciate the work God has done for me. Sometimes our biggest disappointments become our biggest and most cherished blessings.

Remember Our Blessed Lady's words to the servants: "Do whatever he tells you." That's the kind of trust and faithfulness we all need. Then we will, like Mary, experience the power of God working in us.

⟿

Questions for Reflection and Discussion

- Do I trust Jesus enough to do whatever he tells me?

- What can I learn from the relationship the Blessed Mother has with her son, Jesus?

Answering the Questions of Jesus

- How do I respond to spiritual setbacks, when it seems as if the Lord isn't listening?

- How would I respond to this question of Jesus if it were addressed directly to me: "What concern is that to you and to me?"

Question Four

⁓

Why Are You Afraid?
Have You No Faith?

One of the virtues that Christ looked for in all those who would be His disciples was the virtue of faith. This faith, along with the trust that should accompany it, is the theme of this chapter's questions: "Why are you afraid? Have you no faith?" (Mark 4:40).

Faith has two aspects. The first relates to the mind—our intellectual affirmation of the truth. We read in the Letter to the Hebrews that faith is "the conviction of things not seen" (Hebrews 11:1). For example, none of us have seen Heaven yet, but we believe there is a Heaven because we have the revelation of God, including the words of His Son in Scripture. Although we haven't seen it, we have a firm conviction about this truth.

Faith also has a second aspect, this one related to the heart — or, more specifically, the confidence we have to live according to faith. In this sense, faith is like trust. We see this in that same verse from the Letter to the Hebrews: "[F]aith is the assurance of things hoped for." Again, let's take the idea of Heaven. Not only do we believe it exists, but we also have confidence ("assurance") that we will achieve the Kingdom of Heaven with God's grace. When Jesus dealt with people, He wanted them not only to believe in the truths that He taught, but also to have confidence in organizing their lives around those truths.

This trusting aspect of faith, which is very important for our spiritual growth, is like that of a child climbing into the arms of her parents, where she feels confident and secure. So it is with our relationship with God; we place our whole life on the line in the trust that God is not going to let us down.

Jesus had to teach that kind of trust to His disciples. If the people were going to follow Him, they had to trust Him. That's where this story from the Gospel of Mark comes in:

> On that day, when evening had come, he said to them, "Let us go across to the other side." And leaving the crowd, they took him with them, just as he was, in the boat. And other boats were with him. And a great storm of wind arose, and the waves beat into the boat, so that the boat was already filling. But he was in the stern, asleep on the cushion; and they woke him and said to him, "Teacher, do you not care if we perish?" And he awoke and rebuked the wind, and said to the sea, "Peace! Be still!" And the wind ceased, and there was a great calm. He said to them, "Why are you afraid? Have you no faith?" And they were filled with awe, and said to one another, "Who then is this, that even wind and sea obey him?" (Mark 4:35–41)

What a powerful story. When we travel with Jesus, we've got to be ready for anything. It's not always a smooth ride. We get a lot of turbulence along the way. And sometimes we wonder, "Is He asleep when I call out for help?"

What do we do when we have trials? Do we keep our composure? Do we remember to make an act of trust in the Lord's Providence? Do we remember He is always with us, even if He seems to be far away — or even sleeping? Let's look at another famous example of trusting — or not trusting — the Lord on the waters of the Sea of Galilee.

Trusting Jesus

Fear is the enemy of trust; when our fears overwhelm us, we begin to lose our confidence. That was Peter's problem when Jesus invited him to walk on the water:

> And Peter answered him, "Lord, if it is you, bid me come to you on the water." He said, "Come." So Peter got out of the boat and walked on the water and came to Jesus; but when he saw the wind, he was afraid, and beginning to sink he cried out, "Lord, save me." Jesus immediately reached out his hand and caught him, saying to

him, "O man of little faith, why did you doubt?" (Matthew 14:28–31)

Peter is doing fine; he's actually walking on the water. But then he takes his eyes off Jesus and takes account of the wind and the waves. They fill him with such fear that he loses his trust and begins to sink into the water.

What are some of our fears? We all have a fear of the unknown—of the future. How do we deal with those fears? The most important thing is to remember is that the future is in God's hands. We have to know that everything that happens in this world God wants to happen or has permitted to happen. Everything that touches our lives first has to pass through the hands of Jesus.

Sometimes we fear that we're not good enough—even that the Lord may not love us, perhaps due to our past sins or our neglect of the grace God has given us. We have to trust, though, in His mercy, His goodness, and His love.

St. Paul violently persecuted the Church; as he said in his first letter to the Corinthians, "For I am the least of the apostles, unfit to be called an apostle, because I persecuted the church of God. But by the grace of God I am what I am, and his grace toward me was not in vain" (1 Corinthians 15:9–10). We must place our past in God's mercy and goodness, as Paul did.

Let's learn to put our worries about the future in the hands of God as well! Let's learn to realize that He's right there. Will we wake Jesus? Or will we trust that He knows what we're going through, even though He seems to be unconcerned? He still knows what we're going through, and He will not let us be lost.

Padre Pio put it this way: "My past, O Lord, to Your mercy; my present, to Your love; my future to Your providence." All of our lives are fully in the control of Almighty God. We're in His hands day and night, and He is always watching over us — even when it seems as if He's asleep at the switch. And it pleases Him very much to see our trust in Him.

In St. John's Gospel we read about a royal official who comes to Jesus for His help. He has a son who is sick, but he lives about a ten-hour walk away. He wants Jesus to come all the way to his house and lay

His hands on the boy so that he can see Jesus heal him. But Jesus challenges him: "Unless you see signs and wonders you will not believe." After one more plea from the man, Jesus responds, "Go; your son will live" (John 4:48, 50).

The man had to make a decision. Either he was going to try to force Jesus to come with him, or he was going to take Jesus at His word and go home. The man did go home; he had trust, and that trust was blessed. When he got home the next day, he found out that his son had begun to improve right at the moment Jesus was assuring him that the boy would live.

These are the miracles that happen to us when we have trust. But we have to do our part. In the spiritual life, we talk about both grace and nature. Grace is what God gives us; nature is our part in effecting grace in the world because grace works through nature. An essential part of cooperating with the work of Almighty God here on earth, as in any work, is trust.

An old Russian proverb says, "Pray but keep rowing the boat." We certainly need to pray to God to help us, but that doesn't mean we can just sit back and wait for some thunderbolt from Heaven to make everything right. The Lord wants us to work — to make whatever efforts that we can — in the meantime.

We have to pray as if it all depends on God, but work as if it all depends on us. That's the way the saints went through life. We do what we can and trust that God will bless those efforts. God always does most of the work, of course; we contribute just a little bit. But that little bit is essential; remember that He works through our human nature. Therefore, the more we trust in Him and His work, the more He manifests His power in our daily life.

Remember those words at the bottom of the Divine Mercy image: "Jesus, I trust in You." Let that be our prayer every day.

In order for the Lord to become the One who guides our life, all we have to do is place our hand in His. Because of His great love for us, there is nothing that the Lord wants to happen to us that would ever spiritually harm us. At the same time the Lord will not hold back any grace that we need as long as we place our trust in Him. Let us ask for an increase of that trust.

Jesus, I trust in You.

Why Are You Afraid?

≈

Questions for Reflection and Discussion

- Do I trust in Jesus' help when I experience struggles in my life?

- What fears and anxieties do I have that I can place at the feet of Jesus?

- How can I work with God to bring about the change I want to see in my life, my family, and my community?

- How would I respond to this question of Jesus if it were addressed directly to me: "Why are you afraid?"

Question Five

⁀

Who Do Men Say
That the Son of Man Is?

Our Lord was a teacher to His disciples. And like any good teacher, sometimes the Lord had to see what His pupils were learning.

So one day about a year into His public ministry Our Lord takes His disciples aside to ask them two important questions — kind of a midterm exam:

> Now when Jesus came into the district of Cae-
> sarea Philippi, he asked his disciples, "Who
> do men say that the Son of man is?" And
> they said, "Some say John the Baptist, others
> say Elijah, and others Jeremiah or one of the

prophets." He said to them, "But who do you say that I am?" Simon Peter replied, "You are the Christ, the Son of the living God." And Jesus answered him, "Blessed are you, Simon Bar-Jona! For flesh and blood has not revealed this to you, but my Father who is in heaven. And I tell you, you are Peter, and on this rock I will build my church, and the powers of death shall not prevail against it. I will give you the keys of the kingdom of heaven, and whatever you bind on earth shall be bound in heaven, and whatever you loose on earth shall be loosed in heaven." Then he strictly charged the disciples to tell no one that he was the Christ. (Matthew 16:13–20)

This story touches not only on the identity of Jesus as the Son of God, but also on the teaching authority of Peter and the other Apostles. We're going to focus on the first of the two questions in this story in this chapter and the second question in the next. While the questions appear to be similar, we can take different, but important, lessons from each.

Who Do Men Say That the Son of Man Is?

To the first question about who the masses say that Jesus is, He gets several interesting answers — John the Baptist, Elijah, Jeremiah, and a new prophet. But we know, of course, that He was far more than that. He was the Son of God.

This question raises a contemporary concern: the fact that so many people today think of Jesus according to popular perceptions or fads. It's what we might call "survey theology."

The danger with survey theology is that we can create our own image of Jesus. God created us in His image and likeness. He wanted us to be like Him. Our first parents in Eden were tempted by the devil, who convinced them that they would "be like God" (Genesis 3:5). We've always tried to create an image of God in our own likeness. That's what happens with survey theology.

And unfortunately a lot of Catholics draw their idea of Jesus from popular fads. We want to take a look at how we should form our real idea of the Lord. We must draw our understanding of Jesus from what has been revealed to us by the Lord Himself and what the Church teaches.

Answering the Questions of Jesus

The Real Jesus

Let's look at what's happened over the last several decades. Our culture seems to think that Jesus is outdated. Remember the remark of John Lennon back in the '60s: "We're more popular than Jesus Christ." Well, popularity comes and goes. Jesus always has a way of coming back, though, no matter who seems to be on center stage for a while.

We've also seen what I call the "death of God" theology. This is when people say that Jesus wasn't God, but just a nice person, at best an admirable secular philosopher. People write whole books arguing that Jesus never rose from the dead. They say the Apostles got together and made up the story of the Resurrection because they wanted to popularize Jesus' teachings.

Well, first of all, the Gospels make it pretty clear that the Apostles, God bless them, weren't up to such a sophisticated con. Secondly, we know that they suffered incredibly for proclaiming the Resurrection. They were persecuted, scourged, and often executed. They clearly believed what they were preaching.

I remember a story from Russia shortly after the Communists had taken over. They were denouncing religion to the Russian people—a deeply religious people. A Communist official challenged a crowd of Christians to disprove his atheism. A Russian priest went up on the platform and quoted from the Russian liturgy, "Christ is risen, alleluia!" And all the people responded, "He is truly risen. Alleluia!" Faith in the Resurrection of Christ was all they needed to stand up to the Communists. Christ is eternal—Christ yesterday, Christ today, Christ forever.

Another trend in the last few decades is Christ the Superstar—an image of Jesus with no cross, no self-denial, and no self-discipline. The idea is simply that the Apostles and the crowds followed Him as a curiosity, wanting to see what strange things He might do. But Jesus is much more than a superstar. He is the Son of God, and His very life, He tells us, is the way we must follow. He said to the people, "I am the way, and the truth, and the life" (John 14:6). That's why they flocked to Him—not because He was a celebrity.

People get confused over these very secularized notions of Jesus: concepts that are created by the culture or the media, images of God that don't make any demands on our way of life.

Answering the Questions of Jesus

Survey theology has given us a few kinds of modern, incomplete Catholicism. First of all, we have "cafeteria Catholicism," which is picking and choosing what we want to believe and what we don't want to believe. If the Lord gave us His whole revelation, which is necessary for our salvation, we can't just pick and choose what we feel comfortable with. Rather, we have to conform our minds and hearts to what the Lord has taught us and to the teaching authority of the Church through those He has appointed as His representatives.

We also want to avoid "cultural Catholicism." What we should be doing is bringing the gospel and its values into daily life, transforming our culture. For example, our struggle for the sanctity of life is about bringing the Gospel into everyday human living, making people realize that every life has dignity given to it by Almighty God.

What happens with cultural Catholicism is just the opposite: It tries to conform the gospel to the culture. This is how we end up with an oxymoron like "pro-choice Catholics." Letting the culture direct the Church is the essence of survey theology. It's like letting the inmates run the asylum.

A third kind of incomplete Catholicism is a kind of New Age, or "feel good," Catholicism. The God of "feel good" Catholicism makes no uncomfortable demands on our life; He never asks us to take up our cross and follow Him. This isn't the all-powerful, all-loving God of Christianity, but more like a cosmic self-help guru.

Where do we gain our true understanding of Jesus? It has to be through the authentic Magisterium — that is, the teaching authority — of the Church. We can see in the passage from Matthew that Jesus tells Peter he will be the "rock" — the foundation — for His Church. The Pope is the successor of St. Peter, and the bishops are the successors of the Apostles. When they teach in union with the Pope, the Holy Spirit protects them from error and preserves the truths of our Faith — just as Peter was given the insight into Jesus' true identity.

When it comes to teachings on faith and morals that bind the consciences of the faithful, we need — and we have — the assurance that the Holy Spirit is guiding us correctly. If we didn't have that, we'd always be in confusion, and the Lord does not want us to be confused about Who He is or what He wants for us. Indeed, in the very first Christian community formed in Jerusalem right after Pentecost, St. Luke said that the foundation of the unity of the Church is the Apostles' teaching.

There's an old Latin phrase that expresses the way we should think about the truths of the Faith: "In essential things, unity; in nonessential things, liberty; in all things, charity." In other words, we must first share all the fundamentals of the Faith—who Jesus is and what He taught us. That comes through the Scriptures and the Magisterium. Then, once that unity is established, we must be respectful of differences in areas, such as approaches to prayer or the charisms of different religious orders, where there is no single right answer. But in all aspects of our life, we must practice the love of charity.

The Truth is not up for a vote. Who "the men" of our time say the Son of Man is tells us more about our culture than it does about God. It's up to us to recognize the difference, and to bring the whole Truth into everyday life in our society.

Who Do Men Say That the Son of Man Is?

Questions for Reflection and Discussion

- Is my understanding of Jesus based on His revelation and His Church, or on popular culture?

- Do my life and my faith reflect the truth that Jesus died for our sins and was, fully and bodily, raised from the dead?

- Do I trust in the infallible teachings of the Catholic Church in faith and morals?

- How would I respond to this question of Jesus if it were addressed directly to me: "Who do men say that the Son of Man is?"

Question Six

~

But Who Do You Say That I Am?

Last chapter we looked at Jesus taking His disciples to a northern part of Galilee called Caesarea Philippi. There He posed two questions. In the last chapter we looked at the first of those questions, "Who do men say that I am?" Now we will look at the second question: "But who do you say that I am?" (Matthew 16:15).

Jesus doesn't want to know what the Apostles have heard among the crowds; He wants to know what they have come to believe about His identity.

And who speaks up? Peter, whose answer — "You are the Christ, the Son of the living God" — earns the Lord's praise: "Blessed are you, Simon [Son of John]!

For flesh and blood has not revealed this to you, but my Father who is in heaven" (Matthew 16:16–17).

It's at this point that Jesus changes Simon's name to Peter, which is actually a name that didn't previously exist: "You are Peter, and on this rock I will build my church" (Matthew 16:18). Peter, or, in Greek, *Petros*, is a play on the word for "rock," *petra*.

It's on the rock of Peter's confession of Christ's true identity that Jesus said His Church would be built. That's why we recognize the authority of the Holy Father and, moreover, why we believe that the Pope, when he speaks authoritatively on faith and morals for the whole Church, enjoys the gift of infallibility from the Holy Spirit. That is, he is guided so that his teaching will not mislead us, because that would endanger our salvation.

We, too, must answer the question of who Jesus is as if He were addressing it directly to us. Do we really know Jesus personally, not just as an intellectual concept but as a person?

Prayer is certainly one way to get to know the Lord in this personal way — to develop the friendship the Lord wants us to have with Him. At the Last Supper

Jesus said to the Apostles, "No longer do I call you servants, for the servant does not know what his master is doing; but I have called you friends, for all that I have heard from my Father I have made known to you" (John 15:15). Through prayer we enter that beautiful friendship.

Do you seek to know Jesus? Sometimes we are afraid to get too close to Him. We are afraid of what He might ask of us, or what He might tell us about our lives. Sometimes, though, we need to hear the difficult truth. The truth sets us free from our confusion and self-centeredness. And then we can look at Jesus and really see the beauty and the goodness of the Lord, which brings us the happiness for which we were created.

St. Augustine said at the beginning of his *Confessions*, "You have formed us for Yourself, and our hearts are restless till they find rest in You." That's why we want to get to know Him personally and to love and follow Him faithfully. Sure, He might point out things we have to change, but we all have to change in order to grow. Cardinal Newman said, "To live is to change, and to be perfect is to have changed often." We don't change the essentials of our Faith, of course. But we change in the way we respond to God as we grow to know Him and ourselves better.

And we can even see that St. Peter had to undergo a change of mind and heart. Let's pick up right after Jesus has praised him:

> From that time Jesus began to show his disciples that he must go to Jerusalem and suffer many things from the elders and chief priests and scribes, and be killed, and on the third day be raised. And Peter took him and began to rebuke him, saying, "God forbid, Lord! This shall never happen to you." But he turned and said to Peter, "Get behind me, Satan! You are a hindrance to me; for you are not on the side of God, but of men" (Matthew 16:21–23).

Peter had just identified Jesus as the Messiah, the Son of the Living God. And in turn Jesus identified Peter as the rock — the foundation — of the Church. But when Jesus foretells His Passion and suffering, revealing that He's not going to be a glorious earthly Messiah with a great kingdom on earth, Peter pushes back.

Now, for Peter and the rest of the Apostles, what Jesus was saying would have been shocking. The Messiah they expected was a glorious earthly king. He was going to establish the kingdom as it had been under King David and King Solomon—even greater than that. He would drive the Romans out and install his followers in positions of civil authority. But now Jesus is talking about being betrayed by the leaders of the people, handed over to the Romans, and put to death.

So Peter takes Jesus aside and pleads with Him, almost scolding Him for saying that He's going to suffer and die. Jesus sees the eyes of the Apostles on them and realizes that this is a teachable moment. He says to Peter, "Get behind me, Satan! You are thinking the thoughts of men, not of God." In other words, "The Father may have revealed my identity to you, but now you're not open to His plan. You're thinking about what human beings want—earthly power and prestige."

Remember that Satan had tempted Jesus to use His power to do great deeds so that He would become not just the center of attention, but the ruler of a vast domain. What Satan was really trying to do was to lead Jesus away from the Cross. Even though he didn't realize it, Peter was doing the same thing.

Finding Strength in Jesus

All of us have to grow in our understanding of who Jesus is. We can't try to force Him to be something more convenient for us, as St. Peter did. It's one thing simply to say that He's Our Lord, but we have to appreciate that fully.

Jesus is like a mirror that helps us to see who we are, a mirror that will always tell us the truth. What do we learn in this mirror before Christ? First of all, we have to recognize that we are sinners, because if we don't recognize that we are sinners, then we fail to recognize our need for a Savior. He said that He "came to seek and to save the lost," but we have to realize first that we are lost (Luke 19:10).

Secondly, we must remember that we all have weaknesses and that Jesus is our strength. As He told the apostles at the Last Supper, "[A]part from me you can do nothing" (John 15:5). We can't practice any of the virtues of the Christian life without God's grace assisting us. We would fail, and fail miserably.

Peter did. Not only did he try to dissuade Jesus from His mission, but remember that he also denied his friendship with Jesus three times during Our Lord's Passion. We are all weak, and so we need Christ as our strength.

Third, we have to recognize our burdens so that we can accept Jesus' invitation, "Come to me, all who labor and are heavy laden, and I will give you rest" (Matthew 11:28). It's only if we recognize the help we need from Jesus that we can accept that beautiful invitation.

And finally, we have to recognize our pride — our judgmental attitudes and our anger — so that we can learn from Jesus, who said, "[L]earn from me; for I am gentle and lowly in heart" (Matthew 11:29).

It can be very hard to accept these things about ourselves — that we are sinners, that we are weak, that we are burdened, that we can be proud and judgmental and hard on people. But when we accept our faults, Jesus doesn't use them to oppress us; rather, He lifts us out of them. He gives us that truth that will set us free from our burdens, the truth that all of us need if we're going to find true happiness in this world.

We must not close our hearts to Him. It is when we close Jesus out, not when we let Him in, that our burdens become unbearable.

In the end, like Peter and the other Apostles, we all have to answer that question: "Who do you say that I am?" Is Jesus number one in your life? If He's not, you have to reshuffle your priorities, because if Jesus isn't number one, everything is out of order. But if Jesus is number one, everything else will follow from that, because every other love we have — for our families, for our friends, for our communities, and even for ourselves — flows first from love of the Lord.

⤳

Questions for Reflection and Discussion

- Do I have a personal relationship with Jesus Christ?

- Am I afraid of what Jesus might ask of me if I get too close to Him in friendship?

- Have I accepted my failures and shortcomings so that I can benefit from the strength of Jesus?

But Who Do You Say That I Am?

- How would I respond to this question of Jesus if it were addressed directly to me: "Who do you say that I am?"

Question Seven

Will You Also Go Away?

All of Scripture is inspired by God, but some parts stand out in their beauty and teaching power. One of these is the sixth chapter in John's Gospel, in which Jesus says, "I am the living bread which came down from heaven; if any one eats of this bread, he will live for ever; and the bread which I shall give for the life of the world is my flesh" (John 6:51). This teaching, though, wasn't accepted by everyone.

By the end of this chapter Jesus loses many disciples, and he turns to His Apostles and says some of the saddest words He ever spoke: "Will you also go away?" (John 6:67).

The Bread of Life teaching occurs the day after the miracle of the loaves and fishes, when Jesus fed more than five thousand men with five barley loaves and two fish. Naturally, the people wanted to make Jesus a king. Imagine if you had somebody around who could take care of all your food for the rest of your life. You wouldn't have to do another stitch of work! They wanted to make Jesus, in the words of Bishop Sheen, the Bread King.

But Our Lord's Kingdom was not to be an earthly domain. He had to do the Father's will, and that meant His suffering and death on the Cross. By atoning for our sins and destroying the power of death by His Resurrection, He opens the gates of the Kingdom of Heaven — the true Kingdom — that were closed from the time of the fall from grace in the Garden of Eden. So Jesus would be a King, but not in the way the world wanted Him to be.

The day after this miracle, the crowds catch up to Jesus and He begins to deliver his teaching on Himself as the Bread of Life. He starts off by telling the people that they're following Him simply because they had tasted the bread He had multiplied:

Truly, truly, I say to you, you seek me, not because you saw signs, but because you ate your fill of the loaves. Do not labor for the food which perishes, but for the food which endures to eternal life, which the Son of man will give to you; for on him has God the Father set his seal. (John 6:26–27)

Remember the first temptation of Jesus in the desert. He had been fasting for forty days and nights when the devil showed up and said to Him, "If you are the Son of God, command these stones to become loaves of bread." But Jesus resisted that temptation. He would not use His power that way. He responded, "Man shall not live by bread alone, but by every word that proceeds from the mouth of God" (Matthew 4:3–4). That's the idea that Our Lord is communicating to the people who want Him to be the Bread King.

So Jesus takes advantage of the crowds' search for that bread to tell them that His own body and blood is the Eucharist, a spiritual food He would give to them: "[H]e who eats my flesh and drinks my blood has eternal life, and I will raise him up at the last day.

For my flesh is food indeed, and my blood is drink indeed" (John 6:54–55).

Imagine how shocking it would be to hear Jesus insist that His flesh and blood were real food and drink. Naturally, there is murmuring among his followers: "Many of his disciples, when they heard it, said, 'This is a hard saying; who can listen to it?'" Jesus is unaffected by their doubt, rebuking them, "Do you take offense at this? Then what if you were to see the Son of man ascending where he was before?" (John 6:60–62).

In other words, Jesus is telling them that if this teaching on the Eucharist shakes their faith, there's no way they'll be able to handle His Passion and death. This was a turning point in Jesus' mission; He lost many followers who were simply unable to accept the concept of the Eucharist. How do we respond to the difficult teachings of Jesus and His Church? Do we trust in Jesus, or do we try to go our own way?

Staying with Jesus

It's clear from the emphasis Jesus places on the Bread of Life discourse — even to the point of losing disciples — that the Eucharist is central to His message and His mission. There were three types of reaction among Jesus' crowds to this difficult teaching.

The first one was the negative reaction we've already seen. When many of His disciples heard Jesus' teaching, they must have thought about actually eating flesh and blood — that is, cannibalism. That was not what the Lord had in mind, of course. He would give us His flesh and blood under sacramental signs. But many of His followers were put off: "After this many of his disciples drew back and no longer went about with him" (John 6:66). They didn't trust Jesus; they walked away because they wanted to see before they would believe.

A second type of reaction comes from Jesus' apostles, led by St. Peter:

> Jesus said to the twelve, "Will you also go away?" Simon Peter answered him, "Lord, to whom shall we go? You have the words of eternal life; and we have believed, and have come to know, that you are the Holy One of God." Jesus answered them, "Did I not choose you, the twelve, and one of you is a devil?" He spoke of Judas

the son of Simon Iscariot, for he, one of the twelve, was to betray him. (John 6:67–71)

Jesus is telling His Apostles that if they can't handle His teaching on the Eucharist, then they should walk away as well. That's how insistent He is on this teaching. And that's why we say in the Church that the Eucharist is the source and the center of the Christian life.

In response, Peter, acting as a spokesman for the apostles, affirms their faith and trust in Jesus. At this point they probably did not understand how Jesus could possibly feed them with His flesh and blood — just as we don't always understand what Jesus wants from us. Even so, they believed He was the one whom the Father had sent, so they trusted Him. Unlike the disciples who left, they believed without seeing the proof with their own eyes. That faith was rewarded at the Last Supper, when Jesus formally instituted the Eucharist.

But there was a third response, and that was from Judas Iscariot. Despite Peter's proclaiming the Apostles' faith in Jesus' teaching, Judas did not believe in his heart. Bishop Sheen called Judas the "Eucharistic-less priest," a priest who had no time for or devotion to the Eucharist. Judas stayed with Jesus anyway, essentially affirming that he believed in Him even though he no longer did. This insincerity was the seed that led to his betrayal.

How would we respond to that question of Jesus, "Will you also go away?" Well, through the Church we have the faith of Peter to remain united to Jesus even when there are difficult times. None of us can be certain that we will never walk away from Jesus. There have been good people who have left the Church over the centuries. We must remember though, that many people have also returned, and we can, too, if we ever stray.

We need to pray for perseverance. When I was a young brother studying theology, we were told to pray for perseverance in our vocation. And so I pray every day to continue faithfully in my call as a Christian through my Baptism, as a Franciscan friar, and as a priest. And each one of us, according to our situation, should pray for the grace to persevere — the grace never to walk away from Jesus and never to let our hearts become separated from Him by disbelief, insincerity, fear, or selfishness.

Bishop Sheen said at my ordination, "Holiness is like health. It's easy to keep when you've got it. It's difficult to get back if you lose it." We remain spiritually healthy by practicing our Faith and by doing our daily jobs diligently. That is the way we can persevere in our Faith to the very end, using God's grace daily. Every single day, God offers us the grace to know Him, to love Him, and to serve Him ever more faithfully and diligently.

We pass through this life only once. Let us use every opportunity we can to do good, to serve the Lord, and to remain faithful. Let us then reach out to help others find that way to fidelity in Christ, so that they too may share the gift of the Kingdom of Heaven.

Remember, the Eucharist is the foretaste of the heavenly banquet. So let us pray that we will persevere in our love and fidelity to Christ in the Eucharist.

Will You Also Go Away?

~

Questions for Reflection and Discussion

- Do I trust Jesus and His Church even when I struggle to understand His teachings?

- How can I bring God's love and truth to those who have left Jesus?

- What spiritual exercises can I bring into my daily life to maintain my spiritual well-being and my faithfulness to Jesus?

- How would I respond to this question of Jesus if it were addressed directly to me: "Will you also go away?"

Question Eight

～

What Were You
Discussing on the Way?

We're now going to focus on what was likely the most embarrassing question Our Lord had to ask His Apostles. They weren't exactly the A-Team in their response to what Jesus taught them. He had to be very patient, guiding them along step by step.

Let's pick up the Gospel of Mark where Jesus makes His second prediction of the Passion:

> They went on from there and passed through Galilee. And he would not have any one know it; for he was teaching his disciples, saying to them, "The Son of man will be delivered into

the hands of men, and they will kill him; and when he is killed, after three days he will rise." But they did not understand the saying, and they were afraid to ask him. (Mark 9:30–32)

The apostles didn't yet understand the spiritual nature of the Kingdom Jesus was teaching them about. It was a common expectation at the time that the Jewish people would receive a Messiah who would be a very powerful earthly ruler. This was, naturally, the Apostles' expectation as well. Since they believed Jesus was the Messiah they had been anticipating, they expected Him to establish this great earthly kingdom. Jesus had to correct their attitude about what kind of a kingdom He was really talking about. Here's how that passage continues:

And they came to Capernaum; and when he was in the house he asked them, "What were you discussing on the way?" But they were silent; for on the way they had discussed with one another who was the greatest. And he sat down and called the twelve; and he said to them, "If any one would be first, he must be last of all and servant of all." And he took a child, and put him in the midst of them; and taking him in his arms, he said to them, "Whoever receives one such child in my name receives me; and whoever receives me, receives not me but him who sent me." (Mark 9:33–37)

I picture Jesus walking far ahead of the Apostles on the way to Capernaum. We know they were having a conversation that they didn't want Jesus to hear. And when they arrive He gently confronts them. Even though He was out of earshot, He still knew what they were talking about.

Silence.

What an immature situation! It's like a teacher reprimanding elementary-school students. They realized that were arguing like little kids and were dumbfounded by Jesus' question. Even though they were all grown men, spiritually they were quite immature.

The reason these Apostles could not understand Jesus' teaching about His Passion and death is that their hearts were so focused on an earthly kingdom. There was no room in their thinking for a spiritual kingdom. They were, as we all are to varying degrees, ambitious; each wanted to be top dog in this new dispensation. There certainly was no room in their thinking for Jesus' suffering and dying.

But as a good teacher, Jesus knew that this was a learning opportunity. He had to tell them that they must surrender their desire to be number one.

Don't we sometimes experience this ourselves in our dealing with one another? Maybe it's a parish committee or a prayer meeting where we want to be the most recognized, the most important, the most influential. If we want to follow Christ, we have to be willing to abandon that kind of attitude.

St. Paul had to deal with this in Corinth, where the Christian community was divided into factions based on different leaders they admired:

> But I, brethren, could not address you as spiritual men, but as men of the flesh, as babes in Christ. I fed you with milk, not solid food; for you were not ready for it; and even yet you are not ready, for you are still of the flesh. For while there is jealousy and strife among you, are you

not of the flesh, and behaving like ordinary
men? (1 Corinthians 3:1–3)

In other words, he was telling them that the only wisdom they had was the wisdom of the world, rather than
the wisdom of the kingdom of God. He wanted to give
them more substantive spiritual guidance, but because
they were so spiritually immature, they weren't ready
for it.

Isn't that exactly what the Apostles were experi-
encing and arguing about with one another? It should
give us a little consolation if we struggle with the
same problems as Jesus' hand-picked Apostles —and
we all do. It's not how you start off, though, but how
you end up that's most important.

Living with the Spirit of Servanthood

How can we overcome our prideful ambition? Well,
Jesus teaches us the same way He taught the Apostles: "If any one would be first, he must be last of all
and servant of all."

This is a teaching that we find several times throughout the Gospel. Jesus teaches it when James and John

want to be first in the Kingdom, and He repeats it at the Last Supper when He washes the Apostles' feet. We are to make ourselves last and surrender the first place to someone else. It is not the one who exalts himself who is approved by God, but the one whom God exalts.

That's why we need to become servants — servants to others and servants to God. Pope Gregory the Great used as his title "the Servant of the Servants of God." St. Francis never used the word *Superior* for the one who was in charge in his order; He always called the person in charge a servant or guardian — one who protects the community and sees to its good, not an exalted leader.

Are we ready to serve? The Blessed Mother's self-image was as a servant. Remember when she gave her consent to the Archangel Gabriel, "Behold, I am the handmaid of the Lord; let it be to me according to your word" (Luke 1:38). Mary was ready to fulfill God's plan as handmaid. It is precisely in being so humble that she was exalted above every other saint and angel in Heaven.

Jesus also tells us in this reading not only to be servants but to be childlike. The Pharisees — many of whom were hypocritical scholars of the old Jewish law — had no time for children. The Apostles also fell into that error. Remember when the mothers were bringing their little children to Jesus and the Apostles scolded them? Jesus rebuked the Apostles, saying, "Let the children come to me, do not hinder them; for to such belongs the kingdom of God" (Mark 10:14).

We too must be childlike in the way we approach others. We must be sensitive to the least of God's people, and to receive a child symbolizes that readiness to serve the least of the Lord's brothers and sisters. "[A]s you did it to one of the least of these my brethren, you did it to me" (Matthew 25:40).

In our own lives, this question of Jesus could be phrased like this: "What are you thinking and talking about when you think I am not listening?" How would we answer the Lord? Would we be embarrassed into silence like the Apostles?

Maybe ambition or pride has gotten in our way and has kept us from really serving Him in a way that He wants to be served. Are we preoccupied with achieving earthly goods instead of spiritual goods? We need to recognize and understand the spiritual nature of the service we are to give the Lord—that we are really working not for some earthly prize but for the Kingdom of Heaven.

Similarly, would we, like our Blessed Mother, be able to say that we are servants and handmaids of the Lord? St. Paul says, "None of us lives to himself, and none of us dies to himself" (Romans 14:7). While we're alive, we're alive to serve the Lord; when we die, we die as His servants. Are we ready to serve the Lord, ready to carry out all that He wants? Because if we do that, we will focus on what Jesus wants, not on what we want. We'll draw attention to the Lord rather than to ourselves.

St. Teresa of Ávila teaches us that spiritual maturity can be measured by asking ourselves three questions. First, am I doing God's will more faithfully as I discern it in my life? Second, am I bearing sufferings more patiently? Third, am I expanding my love for others? Am I reaching out in love to strangers, to the poor, to sinners, and even to my enemies—those I would never have loved before?

If so, then I have the kind of love that allows me to concern myself only with being more generous and giving to others. That's the kind of love that Jesus was really leading the Apostles to in this Gospel story. When we rejoice at the good of others, we rejoice in the glory of God. We should want good for our brothers and sisters as we want to have that good for ourselves—not for our sake, but for theirs, and therefore for the Lord's.

As St. Paul famously wrote to the Corinthians: "Love is patient and kind; love is not jealous or boastful; ... it does not rejoice at wrong, but rejoices in the right" (1 Corinthians 13:4, 6).

⌒

Questions for Reflection and Discussion

- How can I purify my thoughts and my words, all of which God hears?

- Am I willing to give up prestige in this world for the sake of the true Kingdom of Heaven?

- Do I look to the Blessed Mother for her prayers and guidance in living as a servant of God?

Answering the Questions of Jesus

- How would I respond to this question of Jesus if it were addressed directly to me: "What were you discussing on the way?"

Do You Know What I Have Done to You?

At the Last Supper Jesus knew that He was about to leave the world and return to the Father. And so He wanted to do as much as He could to show the Apostles how He wanted them to grow in the life He had given them.

He was ready to give them awesome powers at the Last Supper, particularly the powers of the priesthood. They would have authority over the care of the Eucharist, one of the greatest responsibilities in the world. Additionally they would have the power to lead the Church with a threefold mission: to sanctify us, to guide us, and to teach us.

He wanted to impress on the Apostles the true spirit with which they should exercise these priestly powers and carry out their mission.

As we have seen, the Apostles were often preoccupied with who among them was the most important. This even arose at the Last Supper. St. Luke records Jesus' response:

> A dispute also arose among them, which of them was to be regarded as the greatest. And [Jesus] said to them, "The kings of the Gentiles exercise lordship over them; and those in authority over them are called benefactors. But not so with you; rather let the greatest among you become as the youngest, and the leader as one who serves. For which is the greater, one who sits at table, or one who serves? Is it not the one who sits at table? But I am among you as one who serves." (Luke 22:24–27)

Jesus was trying to teach them the proper attitude with which to exercise the priestly office — that of servants. And He leaves His own example, giving them a tremendous example of service:

Do You Know What I Have Done to You?

Jesus, knowing that the Father had given all things into his hands, and that he had come from God and was going to God, rose from supper, laid aside his garments, and girded himself with a towel. Then he poured water into a basin, and began to wash the disciples' feet, and to wipe them with the towel with which he was girded.

He came to Simon Peter; and Peter said to him, "Lord, do you wash my feet?" Jesus answered him, "What I am doing you do not know now, but afterward you will understand." Peter said to him, "You shall never wash my feet." Jesus answered him, "If I do not wash you, you have no part in me." Simon Peter said to him, "Lord, not my feet only but also my hands and my head!"

Jesus said to him, "He who has bathed does not need to wash, except for his feet, but he is clean all over; and you are clean, but not all of you." For he knew who was to betray him; that was why he said, "You are not all clean." (John 13:3–11)

Washing feet, it is important to understand, was such a menial task that even Jewish slaves could not be compelled to do it.

Peter had extraordinary authority; Jesus had given him the keys to the Kingdom of Heaven. You can't have more power than that. But He wanted Peter to understand that he had to exercise his authority — his role as head of the Apostles and head of the Church — in the spirit of service, even to the point of lowering himself below the station of a slave.

Jesus then went on to interpret what He had done for His disciples, and that's where we find this chapter's question:

> When he had washed their feet, and taken his garments, and resumed his place, he said to them, "Do you know what I have done to you? You call me Teacher and Lord; and you are right, for so I am. If I then, your Lord and Teacher, have washed your feet, you also ought to wash one another's feet. For I have given you an example, that you also should do as I have done to you." (John 13:12–15)

Jesus gave them an example to follow and to pass on to those who would exercise authority in the Church after them. We're all called to be servants in our own circumstances because we are all members of the Church. We all have the authority and the responsibility to carry out the work of Christ.

Building a Civilization of Love

We can answer Jesus' question — "Do you know what I have done to you?" — in two ways. First of all, we can follow the example of Jesus by performing the corporal and spiritual works of mercy.

The corporal words of mercy are encapsulated in Matthew 25:35–36: "I was hungry and you gave me food, I was thirsty and you gave me drink, I was a stranger and you welcomed me, I was naked and you clothed me, I was sick and you visited me, I was in prison and you came to me." *Corporal* means "bodily," so these are physical ways to spread God's love and mercy to others. We can perform them in so many ways.

Then we also have the lesser-known, spiritual works of mercy, which are just as important:

- *Instructing the ignorant*: we can teach those who need to learn about their Faith and how to live a good Christian life, perhaps through teaching catechism.

- *Admonishing the sinner*: we can warn those who are living out of step with God's will. We should want the best for others, and that means we don't want them to be spiritually lost. We can confront them in a prudent way that moves them to examine their lives without isolating them.

- *Counseling the doubtful*: we can listen kindly and carefully to those who are worried and fearful, helping them to resolve what is troubling them.

- *Forgiving injuries*: we have to learn to forgive one another as Christ taught us by His word and example, especially on the Cross when He prayed, "Father, forgive them; for they know not what they do" (Luke 23:34).

- *Bearing wrongs patiently*: we can let go of little transgressions before resentment builds up inside us. It may be hard for us to put up with somebody else but remember that they have to put up with us, too, including all our faults and quirks, which we may even be blind to.

- *Consoling the sorrowful*: we can reach out to people in times of grief and anxiety to show our concern and to express our sympathy.

- *Praying for the living and the dead*: we can and should pray every day for one another—especially for the conversion of sinners and for the souls in Purgatory.

By performing the corporal and spiritual works of mercy, we will not only be fulfilling Jesus' teaching in this Gospel story but will also be building the "civilization of love" that Pope St. John Paul II, Pope Benedict, and Pope Francis have talked about. Remember the old saying, "It is better to light one candle than to curse the darkness." If we see all the problems in the world and just throw up our hands and walk away, we're avoiding our responsibilities. But if we light one candle, others will be encouraged to do the same. We can change the world, as Mother Teresa would say, one person at a time.

The second way we can answer this question of Jesus is by honestly asking ourselves: What has Jesus done for me? We should look at all the gifts we have, especially the Lord's blessings that we might easily take for granted. Nothing we have really comes from ourselves, except our sins. If God took back everything He gave us, the only thing that would remain would be our sins.

The very first gift we have from God is our existence. God knows all the possible people who could have existed: billions and trillions and more — an infinite variety. But you and I are actually here, while many, many more God never willed into existence.

What about the blessings of our families — the love we share, as well as the security the Lord has given us? Our food and shelter, our upbringing, our education, our talents? We may have talents in music or sports or acting or gardening or cooking. These are all natural gifts from God for which we must be appreciative and which we must put to good use for His glory.

What about the supernatural gifts — the gifts of grace? In our Baptism, we became adopted children of God; we have the life of the Blessed Trinity within us. And then at our Confirmation we became adult Christians. When I was confirmed, we were called "soldiers of Christ," and the bishop gave us a little slap to remind us to stand up for the Faith. We have the gift of Christ living in us. We can say with St. Paul, "It is no longer I who live, but Christ who lives in me" (Galatians 2:20).

Do we appreciate the gifts we've received? Are we ready to use them? Are we ready to go out and spread the message of Christ's love? If so, we're ready to serve. That was the point Our Blessed Lord was making to His Apostles. If we make ourselves humble, we can transform the world.

"Do not be overcome by evil, but overcome evil with good" (Romans 12:21). Hatred is broken down by charity, love, and forgiveness. When we reach out to help one another, we build that civilization of love and truth.

Let us be grateful for the gifts that God has given us, using them every day to make the world a more loving and beautiful place. Then we will be lighting candles rather than cursing the darkness. And pretty soon the whole world will be glowing with the light of Christ.

⁓

Questions for Reflection and Discussion

- Do I look daily to Jesus for His help and His example for how to live?

- How can I practice the spiritual and corporal works of mercy in my life?

- What can I do to show gratitude for what Jesus has done for me?

- How would I respond to this question of Jesus if it were addressed directly to me: "Do you know what I have done to you?"

Question Ten

~

For What Can a Man
Give in Return for His Life?

Bishop Sheen used to say that at the end of our earthly life, we will meet one of two figures: Jesus or Satan. And one of them will say, "You're mine."

The questions we will consider in this chapter are about the choice we have between Jesus and the devil, Heaven and Hell, life and death: "For what does it profit a man, to gain the whole world and forfeit his life? For what can a man give in return for his life?" (Mark 8:36–37).

We need to live with the end of our lives in mind. Heaven will fulfill our every desire. All the happiness, beauty, and joy we can find in this life are but a tiny reflection of the happiness, beauty, and joy of God Himself. Heaven is going to fulfill every hope we've ever had; every dream will come true. And Hell will fulfill every dread we've ever had; every nightmare will come true.

The stakes are high. It's eternal happiness or eternal misery. We have to live each day making sure we follow the way that will lead us to Christ. That's the purpose of Jesus' questions in this chapter.

It can be shocking to hear Our Lord talk about the lengths we should go to in order to see Heaven and avoid Hell. He famously said, "If your right eye causes you to sin, pluck it out and throw it away; it is better that you lose one of your members than that your whole body be thrown into hell" (Matthew 5:29). Now, He doesn't mean for us to do that literally. The point is that there should be nothing in this life that we should be unwilling to sacrifice if it stands in the way of our getting to Heaven.

Vince Lombardi used to say that, in football, winning isn't the main thing; it's the *only* thing. We can adapt that to the Christian life: salvation isn't the main thing; it's the *only* thing.

For What Can a Man Give in Return for His Life?

God created us to be in the Kingdom of Heaven. That's why we're here. The Trinity—God the Father, Son, and Holy Spirit—are perfectly happy for all eternity. God doesn't really need us humans. He created us, though, so that we might share His happiness. Spending eternity in Heaven is the very purpose for which we were created. If we don't reach that goal, we miss the whole reason for our existence. That would be beyond tragic. And that's why Jesus challenges us to live our lives faithfully so that we will be found worthy to enter into His Kingdom.

The world, the flesh, and the devil will give you pleasure. They will give you an illusion of greatness through success and popularity, but it won't be fulfilling. Why? Because the world doesn't give you joy. Joy comes in a commitment to love others so we can participate in the joy of Christ. After all, we were made for Jesus.

The Fruitfulness of Love

Let's take a look at Jesus' teaching here in its entirety:

And he called to him the multitude with his disciples, and said to them, "If any man would come after me, let him deny himself and take up his cross and follow me. For whoever would save his life will lose it; and whoever loses his life for my sake and the gospel's will save it. For what does it profit a man, to gain the whole world and forfeit his life? For what can a man give in return for his life? For whoever is ashamed of me and of my words in this adulterous and sinful generation, of him will the Son of man also be ashamed, when he comes in the glory of his Father with the holy angels." (Mark 8:34–38)

In this passage Jesus tells us that there are three things that a person has to do to join Him in His Kingdom: "deny himself," "take up his cross," and "follow me."

You and I must live the way that God created us to live, not the way our culture wants us to live. That means we have to deny ourselves certain things — first of all, sin. We have to remove from our lives occasions of sin, which are circumstances — people, places, situations — that make us vulnerable to serious sin, even if those things are enjoyable.

Then we have to strive to overcome our sinful habits and to control our passions. St. Paul tells us that the flesh fights against the Holy Spirit within us. If we follow the way the Spirit leads us, practicing and growing in the virtues in our everyday life, we will find peace and will gradually overcome our passions.

Secondly, Jesus says we have to take up our cross. We all have a cross in life, and to take it up means to fulfill our responsibilities and to accept the burdens that come along with those responsibilities. These are different for everyone, depending on our circumstances, our vocation, and so on. As we patiently bear our trials, we learn how to forget ourselves while loving others. The beautiful thing about that love is that, as it grows, it helps us in so many ways. It allows us to take up our cross cheerfully. It makes it easier for us to sacrifice our time and energy for others. In fact, it challenges us to serve more and more. Love, like life itself, is most fruitful when it is given.

Love grows as we give it away but shrinks as we try to keep it for ourselves. The very nature of love is self-giving. When we give our lives in service and in love, we will find more and more love for others and for Christ in our lives.

And finally, the third thing Jesus tells us is simply to follow Him — to follow the example He sets for us. Jesus is the only way: "I am the way, and the truth, and the life" (John 14:6). If we follow anyone else, we will get lost. "I am the light of the world; he who follows me will not walk in darkness" (John 8:12). We need to follow Jesus as the authentic way to salvation.

Yes, there will be sufferings. But remember Jesus' teaching about the grain of wheat: "Unless a grain of wheat falls into the earth and dies, it remains alone; but if it dies, it bears much fruit" (John 12:24). When we die to ourselves by emptying ourselves in the service of others, we will be like that grain of wheat, and the world will be a better place due to a bountiful harvest of grace and goodness for the Church.

This is what the Lord means when He says, in the original passage, "whoever would save his life will lose it; and whoever loses his life for my sake and the gospel's will save it." Anyone who wants to keep his life for himself by refusing to give of himself to help others will finish in the end with nothing. But in dying to ourselves, we become fruitful in Christ.

Let's compare the last words of two Catholic leaders who served under King Henry VIII. Cardinal Thomas Wolsey put his earthly power above his duties to Christ and the Church. He died in great pain, saying, "If I had served God as diligently as I have done the King, He would not have given me over in my grey hairs." While an important figure in his age, Wolsey is remembered more for his failures than his accomplishments. St. Thomas More, however, is remembered to this day as a great saint who put his duties to Christ and the Church first and who was martyred for his devotion. His last words: "I die the king's good servant—but God's first."

Finally, Jesus tells us in this passage that we should not be ashamed of Him. If we are faithful to Jesus, He will return that faithfulness, acknowledging us to His Heavenly Father.

Don't sell out for the promises of the world. When I see Catholic politicians who say they are Catholic but who embrace values that conflict with the gospel, it seems as if they are ashamed of Christ. More than that, it seems as if they're looking for something in this world to exchange for their very soul. We must pray for them.

These temptations affect all of us, though, even if we're not in positions of secular authority. We are constantly asked by our culture to sell out on the gospel for a little money, or a little power, or a little prestige. When we feel that temptation, we must remember that question of Jesus: "For what does it profit a man, to gain the whole world and forfeit his life?"

There is no fair exchange for our eternal happiness.

⤚

Questions for Reflection and Discussion

• Do I go about my everyday life remembering the promise of Heaven and the pains of Hell?

• Do I conscientiously avoid occasions of sin?

• Am I ever ashamed of the gospel, choosing other values and actions that seem more "modern" or "practical"?

For What Can a Man Give in Return for His Life?

• How would I respond to this question of Jesus
  if it were addressed directly to me: "What can
  a man give in return for his life?"

⌒

Could You Not Watch
with Me One Hour?

As we have seen, many of the questions of Jesus include a strong emotional element — sometimes from Jesus, and sometimes from the people He's speaking to. The question we're going to look at in this chapter, though, may be the most devastating of all.

Jesus addresses this question to Peter, James, and John in the Garden of Gethsemane. The Passion of Jesus begins in a sense with His agony in the garden. And the Lord suffered greatly, not physically but interiorly — the anguish of His heart. Here is the passage:

Answering the Questions of Jesus

Then Jesus went with them to a place called Gethsemane, and he said to his disciples, "Sit here, while I go yonder and pray." And taking with him Peter and the two sons of Zebedee, he began to be sorrowful and troubled. Then he said to them, "My soul is very sorrowful, even to death; remain here, and watch with me." And going a little farther he fell on his face and prayed, "My Father, if it be possible, let this cup pass from me; nevertheless, not as I will, but as thou wilt." And he came to the disciples and found them sleeping; and he said to Peter, "So, could you not watch with me one hour? Watch and pray that you may not enter into temptation; the spirit indeed is willing, but the flesh is weak." (Matthew 26:36–41)

We can only imagine the tremendous sorrow Jesus must have been feeling. He loved us and was ready to give His life for us, and yet, in His humanity, He dreaded the sufferings that awaited Him.

At the same time He was conscious of the sins—our sins—that were the cause of His suffering. After all, He was dying to atone for our sins. He was willing to become a victim in our place. He must have also foreseen — and this certainly added to the burden of His sorrow — the many souls for whom He would give His life but who would reject His love and be lost from Him at the end.

All of this no doubt passed before the mind and heart of Jesus as He prayed in agony to the Father. No wonder He wanted these disciples to remain awake with Him. When we go through a hard time, it's such a consolation to know somebody is near us, praying with and for us. And that's what Jesus was asking of these three Apostles.

Jesus had already left the others and surely wanted them to pray as well, but He felt He could depend on these three chosen men who were with Him on Mount Tabor when He was transfigured in glory. They saw His ecstasy on that mountain, but now they see Him in agony in Gethsemane. He looked to them for consolation and strength.

You almost can sense, then, the disappointment that He feels when He sees that they are not able to stay awake. Now, in defense of the Apostles, remember they had come from the Last Supper, where they had had wine during the Passover meal. But as Bishop Sheen used to point out, if you feel you're in danger, you don't sleep. The Apostles apparently did not appreciate the danger of this moment, or the gravity of what was about to happen. And so they slept.

Finding them, Jesus tells them to pray that they will not "enter into temptation." He's telling them that prayer can fortify us against impending dangers and difficulties, whether material or spiritual. When we're faithful to God in prayer, God protects us. He spares us many dangers and difficulties that we would otherwise experience if we didn't pray.

I always feel that when I've given time to the Lord, things in my day seem to go better. There are always trials, of course; Our Lord never says that there won't be. But through prayer we will be spared from some trials we never even noticed, or the Lord will give us the grace to deal with our struggles effectively. And when we fail to pray, we more easily fall into difficulties that we would otherwise have been protected against.

Prayer fortifies us. Our Lord intended that the Apostles, through their prayerfulness, would not only give Him strength but also fortify themselves for the great trial that lay ahead. But Peter, James, and John kept dozing off. Three times the Lord went off to pray an hour at a time, and every time, He came back to find them sleeping.

As the Lord says, "[T]he spirit indeed is willing, but the flesh is weak." We want to serve God faithfully. We want to be close to the Lord. We want to be His good friends. But despite all of these good intentions, we experience weakness — the weakness of the flesh and of our wounded human nature, against which we have to struggle. We need prayer and a spirit of sacrifice and self-denial so that we can become stronger in face of this weakness.

Worldly things so often glitter. The pleasures of the flesh — not just sex but greed and gluttony and so on — are undeniably appealing. And we know that in order to resist them we have to be strong and determined; for that, we need God's grace.

Specifically, we need God's grace to do His will and not simply our own. Prayer is what fortifies us in this struggle between the flesh and the spirit. St. Paul expressed this same struggle: "But I say, walk by the

Spirit, and do not gratify the desires of the flesh. For the desires of the flesh are against the Spirit, and the desires of the Spirit are against the flesh; for these are opposed to each other, to prevent you from doing what you would" (Galatians 5:17–18).

We need to watch and pray as Jesus told the Apostles. When we watch, we try to keep away from occasions of sin, those things that would lead us into doing wrong and falling away from the Lord. Then we need to pray, "Lord, give me the strength to be faithful. Give me the strength, Lord, to do Your will."

"Hour of Power"

In thinking about this question of Jesus, I'd like to connect it to the beautiful devotion of Eucharistic adoration, especially the Holy Hour. Bishop Sheen was very important in promoting the Eucharistic Holy Hour. He said there were three reasons to make a habit of adoration of the Blessed Sacrament.

The first reason is to grow in the friendship of Jesus. Bishop Sheen pointed out that Jesus asked for an hour right in that question to his three chosen Apostles. Can we not give Him, present in the tabernacle or the monstrance, an hour of our time? After all, Jesus is our friend, and friends spend time with one another. What greater friend do we have than Jesus Christ? Jesus would like us to make this hour when we can.

The second reason Bishop Sheen recommended that we make the Holy Hour is for transformation. When we pray in the presence of Jesus, the grace of the Lord affects us. When Our Blessed Lord appeared to St. Faustina with His message of Divine Mercy, she recorded in her diary that the tabernacle is a "throne of mercy" on earth for us. We can go to that "throne of mercy" in the Eucharist any time and pray there to Jesus for the graces we need to live with greater joy and love. After all, what are we doing in the Christian life but returning to Jesus the love He first showed to us?

There are three types of transformation that we must seek through Christ. First, we need to transform our mind and our values into Christ's. St. Paul says, "[W]e have the mind of Christ" (1 Corinthians 2:16). In prayer and adoration we begin to take on the values of Christ; we begin to think the way Christ thought; we begin to look at the world the way Christ looked at the world.

Second, our heart must be transformed. We desire so many unimportant things that clutter our lives and distract us. We need to cleanse our hearts, and there before the Blessed Sacrament we can experience that cleansing.

And finally, even our actions need to be transformed. Many have testified that the face of St. Peter Julian Eymard, the founder of the Blessed Sacrament Fathers, would literally transform into Christ's when he would make his Holy Hours in church. We don't need that kind of external transformation, but we certainly need the internal one.

The third reason Bishop Sheen recommended the Holy Hour is for reparation and intercession. Jesus is offended in so many ways by sins all over the world—especially in the Eucharist. At Fátima the angel taught the little children a prayer "in reparation for the outrages, sacrileges, and indifference by which He is offended." Reparation is really offering our love to make up for the dishonor and offenses committed against Jesus by other people.

As for intercession, Bishop Sheen said that before the Blessed Sacrament we should plead for souls with God, as Padre Pio used to say, "that none would be lost and all would be saved." We can pray, for instance, for people in our family who seem to be drifting away from God. The Blessed Mother said at Fátima that many souls are lost from God "because they have no one to make sacrifices and to pray for them."

Bishop Sheen would call the Eucharistic Holy Hour the "hour of power" that would make his day. And it will make your day, too. It's never a waste of time. Rather, it's a precious gift that the Lord will never forget.

~

Questions for Reflection and Discussion

- Do I make time every day to be with the Lord in prayer, or do I make excuses?

- Do I let worldly things distract me from my focus on Jesus?

Answering the Questions of Jesus

- How can I advance my appreciation for Jesus' presence in the Blessed Sacrament?
- How would I respond to this question of Jesus if it were addressed directly to me: "Could you not watch with me one hour?"

⌐

Do You Love Me?

It is fitting to close with one of the most beautiful questions Jesus asked: "Do you love me?" This is the question we all have to answer.

Let's begin with the passage during the Last Supper in which Jesus foretells Peter's threefold denial:

> And Jesus said to them, "You will all fall away; for it is written, 'I will strike the shepherd, and the sheep will be scattered.' But after I am raised up, I will go before you to Galilee." Peter said to him, "Even though they all fall away, I will not." And Jesus said to him, "Truly, I say to you, this very night, before the cock crows

twice, you will deny me three times." But he said vehemently, "If I must die with you, I will not deny you." And they all said the same. (Mark 14:27–31)

It must have been very hard for Jesus to tell His Apostles — and especially Peter — that they would flee from Him. But Peter pushes back confidently, promising the Lord that even death would not deter him.

The problem is that Peter trusted in *his own* strength, rather than in the Lord's. He put his faith in his good intentions but forgot, as we read in the last chapter, that "the spirit indeed is willing, but the flesh is weak" (Matthew 26:41). Until we are put to the test, we don't how weak we are. That's why Jesus said, "apart from me you can do nothing" (John 15:5) — nothing worthy of salvation, nothing that will further the work of the Kingdom of Heaven. We need God's grace; without that grace we are helpless.

And Peter learned that only too sadly. While Jesus was on trial a servant girl asked him three times if he was one of Jesus' disciples, and he denied it. By the third time he began to curse and swear, insisting, "I do not know this man of whom you speak" (Mark 14:66–71).

Luke's Gospel tells us that at that moment, Jesus, who was on trial before Caiaphas, turned around and looked at Peter. That look, though, wasn't one of exasperation — "Peter, how could you do this?" — but rather one of understanding and mercy. Jesus' glance was conveying to Peter: "Peter, I tried to save you from this moment. I tried to warn you, but you didn't understand. You wouldn't accept it. You were trusting in yourself." The Gospel says that Peter "went out and he wept bitterly" (Luke 22:61–62).

Peter's denial is so important — because he was the rock of the Church — that it's one of the few events described in all four Gospels. Peter remembered his shame for the rest of his life. It is said that from that time on, whenever he heard a rooster crow, he would weep. Then, when he was about to die, he told his executioners that he was unworthy of being executed like his Master, so they crucified him upside down.

Peter never forgot his denial of his Lord. But that doesn't mean that he was not forgiven. After His Resurrection, the Lord gave Peter a chance to atone for his cowardice:

> When they had finished breakfast, Jesus said to Simon Peter, "Simon, son of John, do you love me more than these?" He said to him, "Yes, Lord; you know that I love you." He said to him, "Feed my lambs."
>
> A second time he said to him, "Simon, son of John, do you love me?" He said to him, "Yes, Lord; you know that I love you." He said to him, "Tend my sheep."
>
> He said to him the third time, "Simon, son of John, do you love me?" Peter was grieved because he said to him the third time, "Do you love me?" And he said to him, "Lord, you know everything; you know that I love you." Jesus said to him, "Feed my sheep. (John 21:15–17)

Peter had denied Jesus three times, so Jesus gives Peter three chances to atone for those denials, reaffirming his discipleship. It's a beautiful reconciliation—an opportunity to be worthy once again of his great role as a disciple of Jesus.

In the English translation we miss a very important distinction between the words Jesus and Peter use in this dialogue. When Jesus asks Peter the first time, the Greek translation for the word Jesus uses for *love* is *agape*, which is a complete, self-forgetting, self-sacrificing love. But when Peter answers, the Greek translation is *filia*, which is the love of friendship. This is still a beautiful kind of love, but it's not the all-generous self-giving love of agape. Peter is offering love, but a lesser kind of love than the perfect love Jesus is offering. And the second time Jesus asks, the distinction between *agape* and *filia* remains.

Peter is afraid to say that he has that agape love. He had said at the Last Supper that he was ready to die for Jesus, which would have been an example of agape love. But after having failed so seriously, he was afraid to commit himself again to that kind of love.

But the third time Jesus asks him, the Lord switches to *filia*, saying essentially, "Do you love me with the love of friendship?" Peter is hurt by that third request, but it is necessary to atone for his three denials. He responds using *filia*: "Lord, you know everything; you know that I love you." And Jesus accepts that. And He accepts our love, too. Even when we may not have the most beautiful, total, self-sacrificing, heroic love for Him, He accepts the love that we can give Him.

Love through Service

It's very important to notice two things in this account. First, Jesus does not address Peter as "Peter," but rather with his old name from before he became a disciple of Jesus and affirmed to Him, "You are the Christ, the Son of the living God" (Matthew 16:16). That's when Jesus changed his name from Simon, son of John, to Peter. But now the Lord calls him by his old name because he had denied being His disciple. Hereafter He would restore the name Peter to him.

The second thing we see in this dialogue is that every time Peter expresses his love for Jesus, Jesus gives Peter something to do: "Feed my lambs"; "tend my sheep"; "feed my sheep." Every time we proclaim our love for Jesus, the Lord gives us something to do. There's always a mission with which the Lord will entrust us if we love Him — the mission to carry out His plan in our daily lives.

The role of Peter, as the rock of the Church and the head of the Apostles, would be to take care of all of the Lord's people — to nourish and to serve the faithful. All love leads to service.

Mother Teresa had a saying: "The fruit of silence is prayer; the fruit of prayer is faith; the fruit of faith is love; the fruit of love is service; the fruit of service is peace." When we have silence in our hearts, it will lead to prayer. We will be able to hear God speaking to us, and, in turn, we will be able to speak to God. When we talk to God in prayer, we affirm our faith in Him. We don't see Him, but we believe He's there. Once we have that faith in God, He will move us to love Him and others.

This brings us to part four of Mother Teresa's saying: "The fruit of love is service." Once we love, we have to be ready to serve. When the angel came to the Blessed Mother at the Annunciation and told her of God's plan, she gave her consent. Her love for God shone forth in her willingness to serve Him. That's exactly what was happening between Jesus and Peter.

The Lord tells Peter to act out his love in service to God's people.

And that service puts our hearts at peace. We must be ready to serve the Lord. It is, after all, why God made us. The first four questions of the *Baltimore Catechism* give us just about everything we need to know:

1. Who made us? *God made us.*

2. Who is God? *God is the Supreme Being, infinitely perfect, who made all things and keeps them in existence.*

3. Why did God make us? *God made us to show forth His goodness and to share with us His everlasting happiness in Heaven.*

4. What must we do to gain the happiness of Heaven? *To gain the happiness of Heaven we must know, love, and serve God in this world.*

Peter's reconciliation with Christ should give us courage. In spite of his denial, he is still entrusted with the great work of the Church. We should never use our failures as an excuse to stop trying to serve the Lord. The Lord restores us. He gives us the grace and the strength because we can't do it by ourselves. Like Peter, we begin again.

Pope St. John XXIII said that when we die, the Lord will only ask us one question: "How much did you love me?" We can prepare for answering that question by asking ourselves as if Jesus Himself were addressing us: "Do you love me?"

How would we answer that right now?

"Do you love me?"

That's the question.

Questions for Reflection and Discussion

- Do I rely on a prideful overconfidence in my own spiritual strength, or do I rely on the strength of the Lord?

- How can I demonstrate my love for God and for my neighbor in my everyday life?

- What service opportunities can I seek out in order to glorify God and spread the gospel?

- How would I respond to this question of Jesus if it were addressed directly to me: "Do you love me?"

About the Author

Fr. Andrew Apostoli, CFR

Fr. Andrew Apostoli, CFR, is a founding member of the community of the Franciscan Friars of the Renewal; he also helped to found the Franciscan Sisters of the Renewal. He was ordained a priest by Venerable Archbishop Fulton J. Sheen on March 16, 1967, and is the vice-postulator for Archbishop Sheen's cause for canonization. Over the years he has been active in teaching, in speaking at retreats, conferences, and parish missions, and in giving spiritual direction. He is the well-known author of several books and has presented a number of programs on EWTN, where he currently hosts *Sunday Night Prime*.